# To Be or Not to Be Plain?

# To Be or Not to Be Plain?

*A serious call to Anabaptist cultural integrity*

John D. Martin

SERMON ON THE MOUNT
PUBLISHING

Copyright © 2022
Sermon on the Mount Publishing
The material in this book may be used noncommercially for the advancement of the kingdom of God. Please contact the publisher for permission before using it commercially or on the Internet. Brief quotations in reviews or articles are permitted.

Cover design by Lana Kuhns

ISBN 978-1-68001-036-7

For additional titles and other material by the same author, contact:
**Sermon on the Mount Publishing**
P.O. Box 246
Manchester, MI 48158
(734) 428-0488
the-witness@sbcglobal.net
www.kingdomreading.com

*Our Mission*
To obey the commands of Christ and to teach men to do so.

First Printing—December 2022—1,325 copies
Second Printing—February 2023—7,500 copies

# To Be or Not to Be Plain?

**B**orn in 1946, I lived through the '60s, a time of great rebellion against all institutions and authority. I have seen American society decline into greater and greater decadence. As a teenager, I lived in an American society that accepted traditional cultural norms, and almost all Christians would have spoken out against such things as dancing, movies, the theater, cardplaying, social drinking, divorce and remarriage, and women taking leadership. In my boyhood, I knew of only one man in our whole Greencastle-Antrim, Pennsylvania, community who was divorced and remarried.

I lived to see all of that change. By the end of the century, even though some Christians had fought against the dissolution of marriage, that culture war was lost, and today, most churches have about the same percentage of divorce and remarriage as the world. The remaining cultural norms commonly held by Christians have gone by the wayside as well.

I also lived through the cultural decline of our Anabaptist churches and experienced one very painful church apostasy. If you would visit the church of my youth, you would have to be told that it is a Mennonite church. Nothing about the visible lifestyle of its members distinguishes them as a Gospel alternative to the surrounding society.

In my youth, that congregation had been a very conservative Mennonite church, but many of the members thought culture did not matter. In fact, they believed our distinctive culture was a man-made add-on that stifled true vital spirituality.

## Culture Disclaimed

The church of my early years was a very plain church. However, some of the plainly dressed men in our congregation used tobacco. Too many other members conformed to our plain standards but appeared to be nominal believers without a convincing testimony. This kind of inconsistency

## To Be or Not to Be Plain?

led a certain group of people in the church to disclaim our plain culture. They said it was something we had tacked onto the Gospel and insisted that it actually was militating against true spirituality. According to them, our plain culture not only had very little worth, but actually was in opposition to the things that really matter.

These culture-disclaimers wanted something more vital. They promised that a dynamic, supernatural spiritual experience would emerge if we discarded the obstructive cultural norms we were practicing. These people focused on internal experience and thought a dichotomy (contradiction) existed between outward expressions and inner experience, as if the two were enemies of each other. They maintained that a unity of beliefs was all we needed, and that these tenets of faith would be more vital if each person found his own way of expressing them.

This promised super-spirituality really did sound wonderful. It made sense that if each individual made his own Spirit-filled applications, his experience would be genuine and vital, not a wooden conformity to cultural standards. It would be true spiritual life instead of a lifeless,

# To Be or Not to Be Plain?

imposed form. A unity of belief and principle would replace a deadening uniformity. The great variety in expression and practice would nevertheless demonstrate a unity of belief and principle. We could be more appealing to the world as true Christians expressing a powerful spirituality, unencumbered by lifeless legalism.

But this approach underestimated something—it minimized the subtle temptation of *self-expression*.

Through most of its history, the church feared self-expression because it paved the way to individualism and pride. In general, churches checked self-expression with clearly defined cultural norms. But in my time, the checks on self-expression were discarded, both in society and in the church, and individualism took over. The church of my youth finally found itself pleading in vain against unacceptable individual expressions, and those pleas fell on deaf ears.

But until the breakdown occurred, the voices around me made me wonder if our plain culture was necessary. I wondered why it seemed to take so much culture to make Christianity succeed? I was failing to see what the Apostle Paul plainly understood: that it is the world's culture that militates against true spirituality, not a uniform expression of Gospel applications.

Paul says in Romans 12, "Be not conformed to this world, but be transformed by the renewing of your mind." The very next verse says a person with a transformed mind does not "think of himself more highly than he ought to think." The first evidence of a transformed mind, then, is humility, the opposite of an individualistic expression that calls attention to itself. In fact, this proper view of self is also the best evidence of a genuine new birth, with Jesus on the throne of one's heart and self on the cross.

## A Form of Godliness?

In their criticism of plain culture, many people have quoted Paul's words about those who have "a form of godliness, but deny the power thereof." This glib criticism applies these words to the wrong people. Note the kind of people Paul is actually describing:

> This know also, that in the last days perilous times shall come. For men shall be lovers of their

> own selves, covetous, boasters, proud, blasphemers, disobedient to parents, unthankful, unholy, without natural affection, trucebreakers, false accusers, incontinent, fierce, despisers of those that are good, traitors, heady, high-minded, lovers of pleasures more than lovers of God; Having a form of godliness, but denying the power thereof: from such turn away. For of this sort are they which creep into houses, and lead captive silly women laden with sins, led away with divers lusts, ever learning, and never able to come to the knowledge of the truth. (2 Timothy 3:1–7)

Paul is not talking about traditionalists. He is not describing serious Christians who carefully follow a regulated lifestyle. He is referring to lawless people who have some form of godliness, but deny God's power to deliver them from their own selfish interests, sensuality, and carnality. Today, people quote the phrase "form of godliness" to put down those who are serious in their obedience to Jesus, saying that their show of godliness is only a dead form. However, Paul is actually describing people who rebel against any forms of godliness!

Jesus also targets the deadening influence of ungodliness. He said, "Because iniquity shall abound, the love of many shall wax cold" (Matt. 24:12).

Iniquity is lawlessness, and Jesus identifies *lawlessness*, not legalism, as the reason for spiritual coldness. Let's make sure we target the right "L" word. Jesus never said a unified expression of godliness is a threat to true spirituality. He never criticized the Pharisees for their genuine effort to be holy or for their use of cultural norms. He accused them of being hypocrites, people who tout truth but live for self.

The apostle John in 1 John makes a practical statement about culture. He says, "Love not the world, neither the *things* that are in the world" (1 John 2:15a).

The *things* of the world are tangible expressions. The world is not just about abstract philosophies and ideas. Its ideas take tangible forms, and each of these tangible things is connected to the world's beliefs and values. For example, the casual look we see in the world comes out of an existential philosophy that says, "Do your own thing. Life has no intrinsic meaning, so you just have to be courageous and do your own thing to find your own meaning." Out of that philosophy came the whole casual culture with its demand that "you have to accept me for who I am. I must have the freedom to do my own thing."

People who take this approach insist that they are not worldly because, after all, they are not wearing the world's stressed blue denim that sports rips and holes. But what they are wearing closely mimics the world's existential culture. They do not realize that the philosophy of the world is behind the things of the world, and that those philosophies are not innocent. As the Apostle John warned, they give the nod to worldliness.

Melvin Lehman, a teacher at Faith Builders, recently said, "The effective way to win a culture war is to create a culture, not to fight against the surrounding culture." In essence, he said you cannot win against the world's culture merely by preaching Gospel beliefs and values. You must create a counterculture.

## Culture Demonstrated

The story of the Rechabites, found in Jeremiah 35, is an example showing the establishment and preservation of a distinctive, godly culture.

Jonadab, son of Rechab, helped Jehu to destroy the house of Ahab. He saw the effects of an evil culture, and to spare his family, he countered that evil culture with a distinctive culture.

"We will drink no wine," the Rechabites told the prophet Jeremiah, who had told them to drink wine:

> for Jonadab the son of Rechab our father commanded us, saying, Ye shall drink no wine, neither ye, nor your sons for ever: Neither shall ye build house, nor sow seed, nor plant vineyard, nor have any: but all your days ye shall dwell in tents; that ye may live many days in the land where ye be strangers. Thus have we obeyed the voice of Jonadab the son of Rechab our father in all that he hath charged us, to drink no wine all our days, we, our wives, our sons, nor our daughters; Nor to build houses for us to dwell in: neither have we vineyard, nor field, nor seed: But we have dwelt in tents, and have obeyed, and done according to all that Jonadab our father commanded us. (Jeremiah 35:6–10)

Jonadab gave his family a set of tangible cultural norms to observe forever. We could say they were man-made rules because God never forbade

His people to possess houses, lands, and vineyards. However, He did warn them to be careful not to forget Him when they did have those things (Deut. 8:7–17). Jonadab decided that if a life of settled ease would tempt his descendants to forget God, they would not have those houses, lands, and vineyards. Instead, they would continue to be nomads, living lives dependent on God. He commanded his family to live this way *forever!*

Centuries later, Nebuchadnezzar, king of Babylon, was threatening the land of Judah. Because of this threat, the Rechabites left their nomadic ways and moved into the city of Jerusalem for protection. The Lord instructed the prophet Jeremiah to command these people to drink wine.

Just imagine how easily the Rechabites could have rationalized a decision to accept the wine from Jeremiah. They could have said, "Jonadab instructed us not to drink wine, but that was a law for nomads. We are in the city now. We need to do things like city-dwellers. Besides, the man instructing us to drink wine is the man of God!"

It would have been easy—but the Rechabites did not rationalize away their commitment to the man-made rules of their long-dead ancestor. They would not listen even to God's prophet against the word of their father!

God was pleased with the Rechabites. He rebuked the Israelites because they would not listen to Him and obey, whereas the Rechabites were able to obey the traditions given to them centuries ago by their respected father.

> Thus saith the LORD of hosts, the God of Israel; Because ye have obeyed the commandment of Jonadab your father [not the commandment of God, but the commandment of their father], and kept all his precepts, and done according unto all that he hath commanded you: Therefore thus saith the LORD of hosts, the God of Israel; Jonadab the son of Rechab shall not want a man to stand before me for ever. (Jeremiah 35:18–19)

This account teaches us several things about culture.

1. Jonadab knew God's warning that possessions and a life of ease would tempt his descendants to forget Him. He took the warning very seriously and answered

the danger with a strict but wholesome counterculture.
2. God commended this good cultural mandate.
3. A good cultural heritage is not to be despised.
4. God blesses the posterity that respects a good cultural heritage.

## Culture Defined

Webster defines culture as "a set of *shared* attitudes, values, goals, and practices that characterizes an institution or organization."[1] Notice the word "shared." Allowing each person to express his own view of a group's beliefs is not culture. Culture is *only* what we do together.

I grew up with people who said that if we have unity of beliefs and values, then the practices can be determined by the individual. They thought the church could still be unified because all the different applications would express the same values and principles. This, however, is not cultural

---

1 *Merriam-Webster's Collegiate Dictionary.* (Springfield: Merriam-Webster, Inc., 2020), 304.

integrity. Integrity involves the idea of everything fitting together, with beliefs, values, and practices functioning in one unified whole. In cultures that are unified, a person can see what its people do, hear what they say, see how they dress—in short, look at their whole lifestyle—and discern their values and beliefs.

Another source defines culture as a "term which encompasses the social behavior, institutions, and norms found in human societies, as well as the knowledge, beliefs, arts, laws, customs, capabilities, and *habits* of the individuals in these groups."[2]

## Cultural Integrity

Every church has a culture. The beliefs and practices of a church eventually work their way out in some kind of expression or application. If a visitor to a community sees extravagant houses, cars, and clothes, he would be right in concluding that the community believes material things have ultimate value. The cultural behavior of the community members reveals their value system. On the other hand, if the visitor sees that the people

---

2 "Culture," Wikipedia, accessed November 22, 2022, https://en.wikipedia.org/wiki/Culture

uniformly demonstrate simple dress, houses, and cars, that they spend little on themselves while sending money to support missions and help people in need, he could conclude that the community values the kingdom of God and others more than it values wealth itself.

Cultural integrity means that common tangible practices match what people say they believe and value. Cultural integrity is missing when a group says they have a belief or value, but their practice shows the opposite. This happened in the church of my youth. As its members threw off distinctive cultural norms to chase an elusive "true spirituality," their adopted lifestyle gave the lie to their words. The culture that emerged looked more like the world's values than the Gospel concepts of simplicity and modesty they professed. They had lost their cultural integrity.

## False Dichotomies

In thinking about this subject, many people are misled by false dichotomies. A dichotomy occurs when two positions are mutually exclusive and cannot be reconciled. Good and evil, right and wrong, true and false are dichotomies. They cannot go together; they cannot be reconciled. A false dichotomy occurs when two positions that actually belong together are falsely put in opposition to each other. For example, many people see faith and works as polar opposites that cannot coexist. That is a false dichotomy. According to the Scriptures, faith and works must and can be kept together.

Another example involves missions. Some people believe you cannot have both a faithful church and missions. They think that if you have missions, the church will always apostatize. That is a false dichotomy. God calls for both faithful churches and preaching the Gospel to the whole world.

The false dichotomy about culture is the idea that you cannot have both cultural norms and true spirituality. As with the two previous examples, this is a false dichotomy. We all have seen people with distinctive cultural norms who demonstrate a vital spirituality. In truth, culture and spirituality, like faith and works, can work together, complementing and strengthening each other rather than destroying each other. To be sure, the devil knows the power of keeping the two together, so he does everything he can to keep them apart. However, practicing the two in a vital union can and must be done by God's grace. Pitting the two against each other threatens the destruction of both.

## Cultural Values of the Gospel

What cultural values taught plainly in the Bible grow from a desire to be like Christ and submit to His Lordship? What Gospel values should be expressed by our cultural practices?

*Humility*
Jesus said, "Whosoever therefore shall humble himself as this little child, the same is greatest in the kingdom of heaven" (Matt. 18:4). "Take my yoke upon you, and learn of me; for I am meek and lowly in heart: and ye shall find rest unto your souls" (Matt. 11:29). Paul instructed each of us "not to think of himself more highly than he ought to think" (Rom. 12:3).

*Self-Surrender*
Jesus said, "I can of mine own self do nothing: as I hear, I judge: and my judgment is just; because I seek not mine own will, but the will of the Father which hath sent me" (John

5:30). In the book of John, Jesus emphasized His surrender to His Father's will, how He did nothing, taught nothing, and sought nothing but His Father's will. His attitude was one of self-surrender, not self-expression.

*Equality in the Brotherhood*
Jesus said, "But be not ye called Rabbi: for one is your Master, even Christ; and all ye are brethren. And call no man your father upon the earth: for one is your Father, which is in heaven. Neither be ye called masters: for one is your Master, even Christ. But he that is greatest among you shall be your servant. And whosoever shall exalt himself shall be abased; and he that shall humble himself shall be exalted" (Matt. 23:8–12).

*Separation from the World*
"If ye were of the world, the world would love his own: but because ye are not of the world, but I have chosen you out of the world, therefore the world hateth you" (John 15:19).

*Unity*
"Neither pray I for these alone, but for them also which shall believe on me through their word; That they all may be one; as thou, Father, art in me, and I in thee, that they also may be one in us: that the world may believe that thou hast sent me" (John 17:20–21). While the world celebrates diversity, the Bible tells us to rejoice in unity.

Successful Christian groups throughout history have solidified these Gospel values in the hearts and minds of their believers by common cultural practices.

## CULTURE DEFENDED

As a young man, I struggled with the concept of culture for a long time. I asked people why it takes so much culture to make Christianity work. Is the Holy Spirit not sufficient? Is the Bible not enough?

My difficulty resulted from a misunderstanding of culture. I did not realize that culture grows out of our beliefs and values. It is not an add-on but an outgrowth! Our plain lifestyle was a practical, integral part of our belief in simplicity, humility, modesty, and unity. It rebuked self-expression, individualism, and pride. Our cultural plainness was a practical expression of our belief in modesty and a practical outworking of our belief in *gelassenheit*, a tranquility of spirit that enables submission instead of restless rebellion.

Our plain lifestyle, then, was an outworking of our beliefs and values in actual practice. It served us well in expressing and preserving our Gospel beliefs and values. It helped to keep our Anabaptist people simple, modest, surrendered, and unified while others veered into the world's cultural practices that destroyed the Gospel principles they once held. Our common practices grew out of these Gospel principles, with Gospel principles and practices working together.

If a church attends only to its beliefs without accompanying cultural practices, it will not have cultural integrity, and the result will be self-expression, which breeds pride, individualism, willfulness, disunity, and confusion, the opposite of *gelassenheit*. Astute observers of church history have seen it happen over and over. Finally, serious believers ask, "Why do we have so much individualism, self-expression, and disunity? Why does nobody want to submit to anything? Why does nobody want to hear any word of authority?" Those were the very reprehensible attitudes the plain culture rebuked. The group once had practices that encouraged spiritual values, but they discarded the practices, then found the values disappearing.

Individualism is the opposite of culture because culture is what we do together. If a group says, "We are going to have unified beliefs but let everyone apply them individually," that is not culture. Their cultural integrity has been broken.

This can be an insidious deception because our plain culture gives us a tremendous amount of cultural capital. Therefore, people can start bashing Mennonite culture without seeing any immediate harm. Everybody keeps practicing much the way they always did, not realizing that what they are doing is still based on the cultural norms they imbibed from childhood. This cultural capital allows them to talk with a bold, super-spiritual dismissal of Mennonite culture for about twenty or thirty years before that capital runs out. By that time, the results of their dismantling of Mennonite culture have become evident. The capital is spent, gone, never to be reclaimed. The final result is acculturation to the surrounding practices of the world, with a final obliteration of Gospel beliefs and values purchased at great cost by past generations. How many times does this disastrous experiment have to be repeated before all of us recognize the inevitable tragedy it creates and reject its deceptively pious appeal?

People who disclaim culture often insist that they will never lose practices specifically commanded in the Bible (e.g., the headcovering or nonresistance). After all, these are explicit commands of Scripture! This, too, is a deception. For example, once a woman gets used to every possible arrangement of her hair with a tiny covering, she finally asks, "What am I doing wearing this thing anyway?" The group then restudies the principle and "discovers" that it actually is not taught in the Scriptures after all. I have seen it happen. One step into deliberate disobedience begs for another one, and the group then "restudies" what the Bible says about another practice once thought to be scriptural, perhaps the permanence of marriage. It's a process that can be seen clearly by anyone who wants to see it. Cultural norms break down first, and then a breakdown of Gospel principles eventually follows. Those who disclaim culture assure us that they are serious about learning what the Bible "really says," but their conclusions are suspiciously similar to what they *wanted* to believe and practice.

This approach to church life does not help to win the world either. When I was a boy, the attendance at my church on Sunday mornings averaged about 280 people. It was a large congregation. Today, the Sunday morning attendance in that church is less than half that number. Furthermore, the church does not have a greater proportion of people from non-Mennonite backgrounds than many plain churches do. Their promise that a dismissal of plain culture would win the world proved to be conspicuously false. Not only did they not win the world, but they tragically lost many of their own members to evangelical churches or the world.

What about cultural practices Mennonites consider important that are not explicitly commanded in the Scriptures? Are these just "man-made rules" that should be discarded? I think not. If they are good cultural norms that help us express genuine simplicity, modesty, unity, and *gelassenheit*, must we have a verse to "prove" their validity? For example, most conservative Mennonites forbid alcohol consumption. Although the Bible roundly condemns drunkenness, it does not explicitly forbid all alcohol consumption. However, we require a "man-made rule" of total abstinence because we know alcohol is dangerous and that not touching it is a wholesome practice.

Another example involves musical instruments. Good reasons can be given for banning musical instruments from public worship although the Scriptures have no explicit command against their use. Musical instruments in public worship are known to diminish the pure spiritual experience enjoyed by those who maintain a cappella singing, which is such a wholesome part of plain Anabaptist culture. In fact, the term "a cappella" means "in chapel style," and as a cultural practice, it has a strong historical precedent, beginning with synagogue worship. Although musical instruments were used in temple worship, synagogue singing was unaccompanied. The early church wisely adopted this wholesome worship practice of the synagogue.

## To Be or Not to Be Plain?

Segregated seating is another practice not explicitly commanded in Scripture but commended for its wholesome value. Again, the synagogue had separate seating for the men and women, a practice largely adopted by the early Christian church.

Furthermore, what explicit scripture rules out slacks for women if they are distinctly feminine slacks? After all, both men and women of the Bible wore robes with a gender distinction. On the basis of such rationalization, some who must always have a scripture for a practice consistently have made the decision to allow slacks for women, and we see the result. By prohibiting slacks for women, we are responding to the wisdom of culture, not a direct Bible command.

So then, let's be honest. All conservative Anabaptists maintain any number of practices that they value because, although not commanded by Scripture, they provide good cultural soil for a genuine Gospel experience. The insistence by some that they obey only clear biblical mandates is a very thinly disguised fiction. We actually all agree that some ways of doing things are just wholesome practices learned from a long look at experience and history. That long view helps us maintain highly commended Gospel principles by practices not explicitly commanded in the Bible.

## The Plain Coat

The church of my youth required men to begin wearing a plain coat when they were baptized into the church. I remember how eagerly I anticipated wearing my first plain coat. It identified me with the people of God. I wanted to be part of the church and identify with these plain people.

When I studied at Shippensburg State College, I wore my plain coat to formal occasions. I also wore long-sleeved shirts. In the summer, I was often questioned about these singular cultural practices. Fellow students would ask, "Why are you wearing long sleeves in July?" "Why do you wear that style of coat?" I had many opportunities to present the Gospel beliefs and values they were seeing in my distinctive cultural practices.

My plain coat has served me well. It has never made me feel more spiritual than someone who does not wear it. It has never made me think I was earning favor with God. It has never stifled my passion for true spiritual communion with God.

It has never taken my focus off being Christlike. In fact, it has helped me preserve that focus by giving me a clear sense of who I am and who people expect me to be.

Furthermore, it has given me a sense of solidarity with all the other groups of plain people. Everywhere I go wearing that coat, it declares, "I am one of you." I am not what I am in spite of my plain coat. In many ways, I am who I am because of it. It has helped me focus on Christlikeness and avoid self-expression with its temptation to existentialistic individualism and pride. It has helped me maintain *gelassenheit,* enabling a sense of solidarity with all our conservative Anabaptist groups.

## Colossians 2:20–22

What about Paul's teaching in Colossians 2:20–22 telling us not to be subject to ordinances? Paul says:

> Wherefore if ye be dead with Christ from the rudiments of the world, why, as though living in the world, are ye subject to ordinances, (Touch not; taste not; handle not; Which all are

to perish with the using;) after the commandments and doctrines of men?

Does Paul discourage cultural norms in Colossians 2? If so, then Paul violated his own teaching and so did Peter because they both prescribed rules for clothing (1 Tim. 2:9; 1 Pet. 3:3–4).

To understand what Paul means in this passage, we must look at the context of the entire book. In Colossians, Paul is dealing with Judaizers and Gnostics, who in essence said, "If you don't practice our exact ceremonies, ordinances, and laws, you cannot be saved." Plain Mennonites do not make any such claims for their cultural practices. Various groups have worked out the same Gospel principles in a variety of unified ways but do not seek to impose their exact forms on other groups or claim that others who practice differently are not saved.

A better example would be believers who insist that if you do not baptize with a certain mode of baptism, you cannot be a Christian. That type of thinking is what Paul opposes in Colossians.

# To Be or Not to Be Plain?

## The Pharisees

But didn't Jesus oppose the Pharisees with their many man-made rules? Actually, Jesus endorsed both the authority and commandments of the Pharisees. He said:

> The Pharisees sit in Moses' seat: all therefore whatsoever they bid you observe, that observe and do; but do not ye after their works: for they say and do not. (Matthew 23:3)

Jesus did not condemn even their exaggerated tithing of the smallest spices. He said, "These ye ought to have done, and not to leave the other [weightier matters of the law] undone" (Matt. 23:23). Jesus countered only the hypocrisy of the Pharisees, just as we also oppose the hypocrisy of those who insist on cultural norms but violate the Gospel truths they represent.

The term "Pharisee" means "one who is separated." The Pharisees considered countercultural obedience to the Torah to be the heart of a godly life. Unlike the zealots, they rejected violent revolution and believed that God would overthrow their enemies without them resorting to worldly force.

## To Be or Not to Be Plain?

As we noted, Jesus clearly supported this concept of cultural separation. In His day, such cultural separation was practiced by a very small minority, even as it is today. The Pharisees never numbered more than several thousand in Israel. In contrast to the Pharisees, the Sadducees acculturated with the surrounding Greek society, and by doing so they lost the essential truths of Judaism. This ruling class of Jesus' day, which included many of the priests, had rationalized their beliefs to make their religion fit the surrounding secular culture.

> For the Sadducees say that there is no resurrection, neither angel, nor spirit, but the Pharisees confess both. (Acts 23:8)

The Pharisees had kept alive a belief in the supernatural, whereas the Sadducees, in adopting Greek culture, had become naturalists like their sophisticated Greek neighbors, who scorned "superstitious" belief in the supernatural. For example, Paul's Greek audience at Athens heard his message with apparent receptivity until he spoke of Jesus' resurrection.

# To Be or Not to Be Plain?

> And when they heard of the resurrection of the dead, some mocked. (Acts 17:32)

It is not surprising that Paul had no problem saying, "I am a Pharisee, the son of a Pharisee" (Acts 23:6). He clearly identified with those in his day who, despite their faults, had courageously withstood the surrounding culture to preserve the essential truths of Judaism. He opposed only those who placed their confidence in the culture instead of the reality it expressed. For example, he had no problem with James and his followers at Jerusalem who practiced Jewish culture as long as they did not impose those Jewish practices on Gentile communities as Gospel essentials. Likewise, Mennonites have always viewed Gospel principles as absolute while leaving room for Christian communities with varying cultural norms that distinctly embody those same absolute Gospel principles.

Although many of the Pharisees' leaders were hypocrites, Jesus did not consider their way of life a hindrance to the truth. By preserving the true tenets of Judaism, the cultural norms of the Pharisees actually nurtured a faithful train of redemptionists looking for the Messiah, including Zacharias, Elizabeth, John the Baptist, Joseph, Mary, Simeon, Anna, and the disciples. It is unfortunate that the hypocrisy of the Pharisees' leaders has been used to daub all the Pharisees with the same brush and thereby caricature anybody who is serious about wholesome cultural norms.

## Can We Learn from History?

The Church of the Brethren once defined common cultural practices for their members.

> Traditional Dunkers understood salvation to be a blend of personal faith with participation in a disciplined community of believers. With the proliferation of revivalistic methods, however, individualistic conceptions of salvation gained ground. Brethren began to publicize baptisms, reveling more in the number of dunkings and less in the dunking criteria. Greater emphasis was placed upon one's internal state and less on external submission, escalating uncertainty over Brethren unity and separation.[3]

---

3 Carl F. Bowman, *Brethren Society* (Baltimore: Johns Hopkins University Press, 1995), 322.

# To Be or Not to Be Plain?

The obvious result can now be clearly seen by all Anabaptists contemplating the same course of placing "greater emphasis on one's internal state and less emphasis on external submission" to common cultural practices.

The Quakers also once had clearly defined common practices.

> Quakers admitted that their taboo against ornamentation could not guarantee the experience of the Inward Light, but they believed that requiring plainness brought self-mortification conducive to the type of "tenderness"—or openness—in which one could know God. . . . The ideal was to create a unified Quaker culture so that a plain Friend would always be conscious of his religious distinctness, particularly when in association with non-Friends. . . . The evangelical repudiation of plainness brought a new emphasis on moderation in Quaker material culture called "simplicity," which would be continued by liberals in the twentieth and twenty-first centuries.[4]

---

[4] J. William Frost, "From plainness to simplicity: changing ideals for material culture," in *Quaker Aesthetics*, ed. Emma Jones Lapsansky and Anne A. Verplanck (Philadelphia: University of Pennsylvania Press, 2003), 24, 26, 32.

However, a perceptive Quaker historian asks,

> Has the vagueness in the modern quest of "simplicity" compensated for a loss of sobriety and mortification required by earlier formulations of Quaker plain style?[5]

Before conservative Mennonites choose to follow generalized and vague concepts of individualized simplicity and modesty, they should courageously and honestly answer that question by observing modern-day Quakers.

Finally, we should consider the experience of the Methodists. From the beginning, John Wesley preached Gospel principles without prescribing uniform cultural norms. In the end, he said:

> I am distressed. I know not what to do. I see what I might have done once. I might have said peremptorily and expressly, "Here I am, I and my Bible. I will not, I dare not vary from this Book either in great things or small. I have no power to dispense with one jot or tittle of what is contained therein. I am determined to be a Bible Christian, not almost, but altogether.

---

5  Ibid., 39.

Who will meet me on this ground? Join me on this, or not at all." With regard to dress in particular, I might have been as firm (and I now see it would have been far better) as either the people called Quakers or the Moravian brethren. I might have said, "This is our manner of dress which we know is both scriptural and rational. If you join with us, you are to dress as we do, but you need not join us unless you please." But alas! The time is now past, and what I can do now, I cannot tell.[6]

# Conclusion

Will we learn from the obvious examples of the Quakers, the Church of the Brethren, and the Methodists? Or will we depend on vague notions of Gospel simplicity and modesty and refuse to embrace cultural norms that make a tangible appeal of these virtues to the heart and mind? Will our descendants live with the blessings of a cultural integrity that solidifies common Gospel beliefs and values with common practices? Or will they die with the consequences of a shattered cultural integrity that finally loses the Gospel principles

---

6   *Wesley's Sermons*, Vol. 2 (Dublin, 1789), 439.

once complemented and supported by distinctive cultural norms? As for me and my house, we will choose the precious heritage of Anabaptist cultural integrity.

# For Further Reading

Books which give historical analysis of groups which compromised, then lost, their values.

Bowman, Carl F. *Brethren Society* (Baltimore: Johns Hopkins University Press, 1995).

Fitzkee, Donald R. *Moving Toward the Mainstream: 20th Century Change Among the Brethren of Eastern Pennsylvania* (Intercourse: Good Books, 1995).

Kraybill, Donald. *Passing on the Faith: The Story of a Mennonite School* (Intercourse: Good Books, 2013).

# Also by John D. Martin

*Christopher Dock: Pioneer Christian Schoolmaster on the Skippack*

*Hymns of the Church*

These and many other excellent titles
are available from:

Sermon on the Mount Publishing
P.O. Box 246
Manchester, MI 48158
(734) 428-0488
the-witness@sbcglobal.net
www.kingdomreading.com